Agatha Christie and Ealing

Dr. Jonathan Oates

All correspondence for
Agatha Christie and Ealing
should be addressed to:

Irregular Special Press
Endeavour House
170 Woodland Road
Sawston
Cambridge
CB22 3DX

*****

Overall Copyright © Baker Street Studios Limited, 2024
Text © remains with the author

All rights reserved
Typesetting is in Times New Roman and Rialto fonts

ISBN: 978-1-901091-92-2

Front cover picture: The young Agatha Miller
courtesy of The Christie Archive Trust

*****

All rights reserved. No part of this publication may be reproduced, stored in a retrieval system, or transmitted, in any form or by any means, electronic, mechanical, photocopying, recording or otherwise, without the prior permission of the Irregular Special Press.

*****

Every effort has been made to ensure accuracy, but the publishers do not hold themselves responsible for any consequences that may arise from errors or omissions. Whilst the contents are believed to be correct at the time of going to press, changes may have occurred since that time or will occur during the currency of this publication.

This book is dedicated to
Julia Tubman

CONTENTS

Acknowledgements 6

Introduction 7

Chapter One: Ealing 9

Chapter Two: Mrs. Margaret Miller 19

Chapter Three: Transport in Ealing 31

Chapter Four: Social Life in Ealing 37

Chapter Five: Deaths in the Family 41

Chapter Six: Crime in Fact and Fiction 47

Bibliography 59

Index 61

ACKNOWLEDGEMENTS

The author would like to thank The Christie Archive Trust for giving permission to reproduce pictures shown on the cover and on page 19, as well as assisting with other relevant evidence. Thanks also to Paul Lang for allowing the author to use pictures from his postcard collection. The author is further indebted to Dr. Anna-Lena Berg for reading the text and, as always, providing wise advice. Finally, a big thank you to the editor, Dr. Antony Richards, without whom this work would not exist.

INTRODUCTION

Agatha Christie (1890-1976) is a writer who needs no introduction. She has sold more books than any other writer of fiction. They have been translated into more languages than has Shakespeare and have never been out of print. There are numerous television and film dramas of her detective stories, written from the 1920s to the 1970s, especially those featuring her two major characters, the retired Belgian policeman, Hercule Poirot, and the elderly English spinster, Miss Jane Marple.

The locations in England associated with Agatha Christie are Torquay, where she was born in 1890 and her later homes; Greenaway in Devon and more modest dwellings in Sunningdale and Wallingford in Berkshire, as well as the scene of her reappearance in 1926, Harrogate. Less well known is Ealing; some of her biographers, such as, most recently, Laura Thompson, never even mention it in connection with her. However, Ealing should not be forgotten. Agatha refers to Ealing several times in her autobiography. Peter Hounsell's *Ealing A-Z* has a section about her. A talk I gave about Ealing as an Anglo-Indian suburb in the late nineteenth century referred to her autobiography. The connection is that she was a frequent visitor to Ealing in her youth at the turn of the twentieth century where she stayed with her 'grandmother', the inspiration for Miss Marple. But there is more to it than this, and I will be exploring three topics. Who was the woman that Agatha stayed with? How did Agatha see Ealing? What influences did Ealing have on her stories? Firstly, though, we should begin with Ealing itself, a place known to most people – if at all – for the film studios established on Ealing Green in 1910, best known for the Ealing Comedies of 1948-1955, and still the longest running film studios in the world. There is more to Ealing than the studios, however, as important as they were and are.

In her autobiography, Agatha Christie talks about her time in Ealing. As she wrote, 'Ashfield was home and accepted as such; Ealing, however, was an excitement. It had all the romance of a foreign country'.[1] She often visited Ealing from the 1890s to 1914.

---

[1] Agatha Christie, *An Autobiography*, (1977), p. 38.

CHAPTER ONE
EALING

Ealing's history can be read about in Peter Hounsell's *Ealing and Hanwell Past* (1991) and in the author's *Ealing: A Concise History* (2014) to name but two. There are also several books showing Ealing in old photographs, as well as a number of older histories. What follows is a concise history of Ealing to those who are unfamiliar with it, focussing on the decades when it was familiar to Agatha.

Ealing was described as being 'a country town near London' in 1904. It had existed as a settlement since Saxon times as Gillingas at the end of the seventh century and was part of the manor of Fulham in the Domesday book in 1086. Its parish church of St. Mary's was established in the thirteenth century but was rebuilt in the 1730s and substantially remodelled in 1866-1873. Ealing was seven miles to the west of Tyburn in London and was part of the county of Middlesex. In 1599 it had a population of 428 people. Until 1863 it was the name given to both Brentford, an important and crowded Thameside town, and Ealing proper.

The village of Ealing was made of a number of distinct hamlets; Little Ealing to the south, West Ealing, Pitshanger Farm and Castlebar to the north and the main settlement to the south of the Uxbridge Road around the parish church.

[Postcard image (courtesy of Paul Lang) of St. Mary's church, Ealing]

There were also a number of inns and a few houses straddling the main road. Eighteenth century Ealing saw the parish as the home of many well to do residents, such as generals and a royal doctor, and even royalty such as Princess Amelia and later Edward Augustus, Duke of Kent. In 1801-1803, John Soane rebuilt the manor house, calling it Pitzhanger Manor; Spencer Perceval, Prime Minister, lived at Elm Grove, Ealing in 1809-1812 and there was the Great Ealing school which educated John Henry Newman. America's ambassador, John Quincey Adams, lived here in 1815-1817. Population at this time (1801-1811) was a little over 2,000.

In the nineteenth century expansion was rapid, which was in part due to improved transport links, as will be seen later. The centre of the parish began to shift northwards along the Uxbridge Road. The parish's second Anglican church, Christ Church, was built there in 1852 as was the Wesleyan Methodist church. The town's principal shopping streets; The Mall, Ealing Broadway and the High Street were all to be found here. When the Ealing Local Board had permanent offices built they were first located in the Mall from 1874, and then from 1888 in the larger town hall further westwards on the new Broadway.

Housing was also built along the Uxbridge Road, mostly detached houses with gardens to their rear. Along Castlebar Road to the north were also a number of large Victorian houses. Working class terraced houses were located between the Broadway and the High Street and in West Ealing, known as Steven's Town after their builder, out of sight of the more middle-class residents.

The population expanded considerably. In 1861 there were 5,064 inhabitants, rising to 9,959 in 1871, 15,674 in 1881 and 23, 787 in 1891. In other words, in 30 years the population had quadrupled, and as we shall soon see, change was even more dramatic in the next two decades. This was partly due to falling death rates (15.8 per 1,000 in 1877 to 10.9 per 1000 in 1888) and rising birth rates (double that of the death rates) and people living longer (68 people died aged over 65 in 1888 and 106 did so in 1898), but more so to people arriving from outside to swell local numbers. Better drinking water and health care also helped, as the council appointed a medical officer of health to monitor and improve the situation.

In order to serve the needs of these rising numbers of people, public services altered dramatically. At the beginning of the century Ealing had been administered, as it had since Tudor time, by the parish vestry, made up of unelected members which paid a small number of officers to collect parish rates and to spend them on statutory services; the maintenance of the church and roads and most expensively, to care for the parish poor. This occurred in the small workhouse opposite the parish church. One of their later tasks was to establish a cemetery in south Ealing because the churchyard was full, as was the case with many parishes in or near London, whose populations were rising at an unprecedented rate. This cemetery played a role in Agatha's life as we shall soon see.

In 1863 the vestry's powers, already curtailed by the 1834 New Poor Law which transferred the responsibility of the poor to the Brentford Guardians and their union workhouse in Isleworth, were reduced yet further. The division of Brentford and Ealing led to the creation of the Ealing Local Board. This was a group of elected councillors who levied rates on the population and paid officials to do their bidding. At first these amounted to two; the clerk and the surveyor. The second was responsible for the creation of an improved infrastructure. Principally this was to have proper lighting, roads and sewers laid out. The man who took this job was Charles Jones (1830-1913) and he was to remain in this post until his death. He also designed numerous prominent buildings including churches, schools and the town hall, all of which still stand.

[Memorial to Charles Jones (image © Dr. Jonathan Oates)]

The increase in population and building led to many fine old mansions being demolished. These included Ealing Park, once visited by Queen Victoria, Elm Grove, after it had been used as a school and an asylum, and Fordhook, once home to Henry Fielding. The Hall, former residence of Spencer Walpole, M.P., was demolished. Smaller houses were built in their stead. However, some open land was preserved by the council for the public. In 1880 the first purpose designed park was opened; Lammas Park, of 25 acres, and laid out with tennis and croquet pitches. Land belonging to the manor of London was administered by the council from 1881; notably Ealing Common (47 acres), Haven Green (7 acres), Drayton Green (4 acres) and Ealing Green (4 acres). In 1899 the Manor House and grounds were bought for £40,000 and the former became Ealing's public library from 1901-1984; its grounds were opened as Walpole Park of 30 acres.[1] Another old house, dating back to the early eighteenth century, was Rochester House on Little Ealing Lane, which survived by being used for educational purposes.

By the 1890s and 1900s Ealing was a town in its own right. In 1901 it became the first district in Middlesex to become an incorporated borough with a mayor, aldermen, coat of arms and motto (*Respice, Prospice*) and more importantly, additional powers. From 1903 the council began to build its own schools as provision in existing church and charity schools was deemed inadequate because of their small size faced with a population explosion, though many remained and were expanded.

There were two hospitals in Ealing in Agatha's time. There was the cottage hospital at the top of Northfields Avenue, established in 1871 and expanded subsequently. It was funded by subscriptions to pay for the staff and medicines, though local doctors gave their part time assistance for free. In 1911 a new and larger hospital was built on the west end of Mattock Lane and called the King Edward Memorial Hospital. There was also an isolation hospital funded jointly with Chiswick near to the cemetery to deal with cases of infectious diseases.[2] In 1930 a nurse there was shot dead there by her controlling father, who immediately ended his own life, too. There were, of course, a great many other doctors in Ealing.

There was also an expansion of church building in the Victorian and Edwardian age. Apart from the parish church and Christ Church, there was St. James' and St. John's (consecrated in 1876) to the west, St. Peter's and St. Stephen's to the north and St. Matthew's to the east (consecrated in 1884). St. Saviour's was built on The Grove and St. Luke's to the north west.[3]

Although the established Church was predominant in Ealing there were also a number of chapels built, and there was no disharmony between the two. The Congregational church in Ealing Green was rebuilt in 1860 by Jones, in one of his early commissions. St. Andrew's Presbyterian church was built in 1886-1887 and nearby, just to the north of Haven Green was a Baptist church, built in 1880 in addition to the one on Chapel Road from 1865. In 1869 the Wesleyan church was consecrated on the Mall and in West Ealing a Primitive Methodist chapel was established.[4] Unremarked by Jones was a Catholic chapel on Mattock Lane, which was superseded by St. Benedict's, which was run by monks, but not without a good deal of controversy as the original parish priest refused to obey his bishop in acknowledging the authority of the new parish.

Several of these churches and chapels had schools attached to them. St. Benedict's became a well-known private school. There were also a number of

---

[1] Charles Jones, *Ealing: A Decade of Progress, 1901-11*, (1911), in section titled *Maps of Ealing Parks and Recreation Grounds*.
[2] Charles Jones, *Ealing: From Village to Corporate Town*, (1901), pp. 51-56.
[3] Ibid, pp. 94-97.
[4] Ibid, pp. 97-103.

Chapter One: Ealing

other private schools, some very small, but some rather larger. There was the older Great Ealing School off St. Mary's Road, but there were others; Durston House being one such. The Princess Helena School for girls was relocated to north Ealing and one of its most famous pupils was Dorothea Chambers, a vicar's daughter, who won the Ladies' singles at Wimbledon seven times prior to the First World War. The Heidelberg School on Castlebar Road was another private school for girls, boarders and day pupils, initially run by three sisters aided by their father. Less socially prominent was the charitable Girls' Home in south Ealing, from 1867, for orphaned girls, to teach them useful trades. There was a similar school run by Catholics in west Ealing.[5]

The decade 1901-1911 saw the greatest changes in Ealing's history. Population and housing almost doubled. In 1891, 145 new shops and houses were erected in Ealing; in 1901 there were 637 new buildings, 522 of them being houses. Between 1901 and 1911, 6,912 buildings were erected in the borough. Population rose from 33,031 to 61,235 (of which 6,911 were children of school age) in these years, and Jones attributed this to improvements in transport, namely the trams.

In the north of the borough a new suburb was built; the Brentham estate, a co-partnership development mainly aimed at the Liberal middle-class. Nearby Pitshanger Farm was demolished and Pitshanger Lane was developed as a shopping street with houses, schools and churches to follow. But it was the south of Ealing which saw most change. The land to the west and east of Northfields Lane and towards Little Ealing was open fields until the turn of the twentieth century but in the next decade these fields were all built upon.

The only council houses in the borough in this period were built in 1899-1901 on land bordering South Ealing Road and Pope's Lane. Some councillors and ratepayers were opposed to the council spending money where they thought it unnecessary. They were called Workmen's Cottages, consisting of 131 houses and flats, and were initially only let to men who had permanent employment.[6]

The shops in Ealing had by the turn of the twentieth century become far more sophisticated than they had been a century or even half a century before. Sanders' and Sayer's department stores were prominent on Ealing Broadway. *Ealing illustrated* in 1893 stated 'The commercial part of the town is very compact and the thoroughfares being wide and well lit, they form very agreeable promenades by daylight or in the evening'.[7]

So great was this rate of building that measures had to be taken to save some of the open land for recreation purposes. In the north of the borough, to the west and north of Pitshanger Lane was Pitshanger Park which went as far north as

---

[5] Ibid, pp. 112-113.
[6] Charles Jones, *Ealing: A Decade of Progress, 1901-11,* (1911), pp. 66-67.
[7] Anon, *Ealing Illustrated,* (1893), p. 5.

the river Brent and was eventually the largest park in the borough, initially being 26 acres. Smaller parks were established at Hanger Hill to the north east of the borough and at Dean Gardens to the west, of five acres and three respectively. By 1911 there were 158 acres of open space in the borough. Improvements were made in these parks; park keeper's lodges, public toilets, grounds laid out for games (tennis, croquet, cricket and bowling) and shrubbery and flowers planted. Ponds were constructed in Walpole Park in 1904-1905 as an unemployment relief scheme.[8]

[Postcard image (courtesy of Paul Lang) of Ealing Broadway stations (top) and Ealing Common (bottom)]

There was also electric lighting in Ealing from the 1890s. Rather than relying on private companies, the corporation decided to run its own electricity service. In 1894-1895 there were over 5,000 such lights in homes in the borough. Street lighting remained a mixture of gas and electric lighting in the 1900s. By 1911 there were 883 gas lamps and 935 electrical ones, having increased in number by 67% during the decade.[9]

Politically, during 1890-1914, Ealing was the name given to the Parliamentary constituency which also included Acton and Chiswick, to its east and south east. From 1890-1906 the M.P. was Lord George Hamilton, who was once Secretary of State for India. He was replaced by Sir Herbert Nield, a Hampstead barrister, who was to remain the M.P. until he retired in 1929. Both

---

[8] Charles Jones, *Ealing: A Decade of Progress, 1901-11*, (1911), pp. 40-44.
[9] Ibid, pp. 10, 74-76.

Chapter One: Ealing

were Conservatives, and despite challenges from Maurice Hulbert of the Liberal party in this period, it was a safe Conservative seat, even in 1906 the year of the national Liberal landslide. There were no Labour councillors in Ealing until 1917. Clubs for Conservatives and Liberal supporters were established in Ealing and elections were great social as well as political occasions where many turned out in the streets or at political meetings and hustings.

In the 1890s, apart from the tram controversy, there was also the issue as to whether Ealing should be incorporated as a borough. Some councillors were in favour, but the council as a whole was divided, fearing that it meant an increase in rates, and opposition came from the Middlesex County Council who did not wish to see a diminishing of its powers (local government services being provided at both local and county level). The issue was not decided until a government enquiry had taken place. The charter was granted on the 3rd June 1901. Sir Edward Montagu Nelson, chairman of the former council, was the borough's charter mayor. As regards the council, there were six wards, each returning three councillors, all of whom were male in this era, despite there being a small number of female candidates. However, on the council's committees there were some women as committee members did not always have to be councillors and there were also some female Poor Law Guardians representing Ealing on the Brentford Union.

Ealing was promoted as an attractive place in which to dwell, especially for the middle-class. It had more servants per population than elsewhere in 'greater London' except Kensington. In 1901 there were 4,616 female servants in Ealing, as domestic service was the single largest employer of women at this time and helped to create an imbalance between the sexes of 20,014 women and 13,013 men. In the 1890s a live in female servant could be paid £14 per annum plus board and lodgings and expect a half day off each week. Few of the servants were as unfortunate as Sarah Higgs, found pregnant and floating in the canal in nearby Yiewsley in early 1895, and whose murderer was never found.

The book, *Ealing Illustrated*, published in 1893, sought to boast of the place's attractions, stating:

> 'Few will deny that Ealing is to the chance visitor, a most attractive place. Pleasantly situated amidst surroundings of a charming rusticity, having no spot within its boundaries from which the eye cannot light on refreshing foliage or verdure, and possessing withal every advantage of modern civilisation to the full, it is an ideal residence for him whom the ceaseless chatter of a mighty city wearies, but at the same time the unrelieved monotony of country life pure and simple palls'.[10]

---

[10] Anon, *Ealing Illustrated*, (1893), p. 3.

It was also seen as a very healthy place and guide books often stressed the low death rates. This was nothing new, since Henry Fielding moved from London to his house in Ealing for the good of his health in 1753. On the 9th May 1901 Frederick Miller, Agatha's father wrote to his wife from Torquay in a similar vein about their youngest daughter:

> 'I was much distressed to learn by your letter this morning that Agatha was not doing as well as you could wish and that her fever had not yet left her and I could perfectly understand your wish to get her out of the house and to Ealing. Your telegram just rec'd has greatly relieved my mind for I am sure she will greatly improve at Ealing'.

He added:

> 'Who will you call in at Ealing if you need a doctor? I hope you will not need one for I think the pure air will soon put her right again and I hope to see you both early next week'.[11]

There were, of course, plenty of doctors who Agatha could have been taken to in Ealing and presumably her elderly auntie-granny would have known at least one for her own ailments. There was also the alleged lack of any negative features:

> 'The fact that there are no manufactories carried on in the town adds very much to its desirability as a place of residence'.

In the next decade there was a similar remark:

> 'Ealing has its negative as well as positive attractions. It has successfully resisted all attempts to make it a dumping ground for London's nuisances. It has no workhouse within its boundaries, no poor law schools, no lunatic asylums, and its police cases go to Brentford to be tried and there is no manufacturing element'.[12]

Towards the end of that decade there were diverging opinions about Ealing. That there had been change was expressed by Walter Jerrod, writing in 1909:

> 'The old place has become renewed, and with its residential byways spreading northwards towards the Brent, and southwards towards Brentford, it has a little left of the old time character when it was a village of large houses and wide stately grounds … Thanks to the broad bit of common it is in a way cut off from Acton to the east, but expansion to the west has made it merge with Hanwell and where not many years ago used to be a fairly attractive stretch of highway, now humming with electric

---

[11] Letter from Frederick to Clara Miller, 9th May 1901, The Agatha Christie Archive.
[12] Anon, *Ealing: A County Town near London,* (1904), p. 15.

Chapter One: Ealing

trams pass through rows of substantial villas and stretches of showy shops'.[13]

Another contemporary was C.G. Harper and he was impressed with Ealing:

'I do not think there can anywhere be a more eminently respectable and residential suburb than Ealing. It impresses me with those two qualities in a superlative degree. You come to it by road past a fine common that is almost park like, or else alight at its railway stations, that are not as other stations, but particularly smart, roomy and well groomed, and thence you emerge on busy streets of extremely prosperous shops, and then come to great areas of villa residence built and maintained in good style, the supporters of these shops'.[14]

[Postcard image (courtesy of Paul Lang) of Ealing Common]

Ealing was known by some as the Queen of the Suburbs, a term that is occasionally still used. It seems to have been coined by Jones in his memoir, *Ealing: From Village to Corporate Town*, published in 1901, for it is not mentioned in Edith Jackson's *Annals of Ealing*, published in 1898 and the first full length history of Ealing. He wrote:

'Ealing – the only Corporate Town in the important County of Middlesex, and the first to receive a Royal Charter from our Gracious King Edward VII – enjoys this distinction, and it is no small gratification to know that the once comparatively unknown village is recognised as

---

[13] Jerrold, cited in Jonathan Oates, *Ealing: A Concise History*, (2014), p. 78.
[14] Charles G. Harper, *Rural Nooks Round London* (1907), cited in Jonathan Oates, *Ealing: A Concise History*, (2014), p. 78.

Queen of Suburbs, with a name that stands out, far and near, for its advances in sanitary work, and the retention to the fullest extent of its floriculture and sylvan beauty'.[15]

In 1911 Jones made the additional remark:

'The residents of Ealing, individually and collectively, are proud of the title 'Queen of Suburbs', so often and deservedly applied to the Borough, and the cognomen 'Leafy Ealing'.[16]

Yet it was not original phrase; both Surbiton and Richmond in north Surrey had had it already used of them in the late nineteenth century and so it is probable that Jones borrowed it from them, without any acknowledgement. For Ealing the term stuck; Jones used it again in the second volume of memoirs a decade later and it was used in guide books and directories for some decades to come; in 1991 a council guide made use of it.

Perhaps it is appropriate that the Queen of the Suburbs and the Queen of Crime are so inter-connected. Now that we know a little about the place, we can turn to why Agatha was linked to Ealing and for this we turn to a member of her family.

---

[15] Charles Jones, *Ealing: From Village to Corporate Town* (1901), p. 8.
[16] Charles Jones, *Ealing: A Decade of Progress, 1901-11* (1911), p. 40.

CHAPTER TWO
MRS. MARGARET MILLER

[Auntie-Grannie in old age (image © The Christie Archive Trust)]

One of Agatha's mother's aunts lived in Ealing, also referred to as her grandmother, because she was also her father's stepmother and the composite term Auntie-Grannie describes her the best. Her name was Mrs. Clarissa Margaret Miller. She was born in Chichester in 1828 and was baptised there on the 6th January 1829 as Margaret L. West. She later lived with her uncle at the George Hotel on Portsmouth High Street and was employed as a hotel housekeeper for some years. In 1863 she married an American from New York, Nathaniel Frary Miller, a wealthy widower with a son and business interests in Manchester and who was rather older than herself. It was not apparently a romantic affair, and in any case it was a short lived marriage for he died in 1869 and was buried in New York. The couple, who were childless themselves, may well have lived in the U.S.A. for a few years. It left Margaret as a well-off widow.

After her widowhood Mrs. Miller lived off her investments as an annuitant. Initially she lived in Timperley, Cheshire, in a house her husband had bought shortly before he died. Her sister, Mary Ann Boehmer, was impoverished when her husband had died and had four children to look after. Mrs. Miller offered to take one of the children to live with her – the only daughter – and that is why Clarissa, born in 1854 was living with Mrs. Miller by 1871. However, it seems that Mrs. Miller never loved her, and Clarissa always believed that she was obliged to be forever grateful to her aunt, but Mrs. Miller did later grieve over the death of her stepson Frederick. In 1871 she stated that her favourite virtue was self-denial and that her chief characteristic was obstinacy. If she was not herself, she would want to be a better individual. She may also have been financially astute – or lucky – when it came to money, for she sold the shares she had in her late husband's business, which her sister's daughter did not. The business crashed in 1913, creating problems for Clarissa who lost that part of her income.

In 1881, just after moving to Ealing, she was living with her niece, Clarissa, who was to be Agatha's mother, then aged 27 and born in Dublin. There was her late husband's son from his first wife, Frederick, born in New York and aged 34 (and Agatha's father; he had married Clarissa in 1878 in Kensington), and their daughter, Margaret, aged 2 and born in Torquay and her baby brother, Louis from New York. There were four servants; Hannah Dyson and Julie Adams as well as a housemaid and a maidservant.[1]

Mrs Miller is not listed in the Ealing and Hanwell directory of 1881, which was compiled towards the end of 1880, yet as noted she was listed in the 1881 census, taken in early 1881 and so this must be the latest time of her arrival in Ealing. Ealing, 'which was then still practically in the country. As she often said, there were fields all around'.[2] Yet when Agatha began to visit in the 1890s, 'this seemed hard to believe. Rows of neat houses spread in every direction', as has already been noted. It was rapidly expanding in the late nineteenth and

---

[1] Census, 1881.
[2] Agatha Christie, *An Autobiography*, (1977), p. 39.

early twentieth centuries for a variety of reasons. It was near London, it had good transport links with the capital it had open space on which to build and it had low death rates.

[Postcard image (courtesy of Paul Lang) of St. Stephen's church, Ealing]

But Ealing was still not entirely built up in the 1890s. In 1895 Agatha remembered a field of buttercups near the newly built St. Stephen's church. She and her nurse were walking up a hill near the church and there 'was nothing but fields, and we came to one special field, crammed with golden buttercups. We went to it – that I do know – quite often … the loveliness of it I do remember and feel'.³ By 1914 these fields had been built upon. St. Stephen's church was built at the cost of £6,000 and was consecrated on the 3rd June 1876. Jones described it thus, 'Of these, certainly in architectural beauty, stands out prominently the church of St. Stephen. Occupying one of the most commanding positions in Ealing, it forms a landmark, and makes as prominent a feature as its northern neighbour on Harrow Hill'.⁴

[Copy of part of the OS map of central Ealing in 1914. The arrow points to No. 9 Craven Gardens, home to Mrs. Miller, from 1881-1914]

Mrs Miller and her household lived at the newly built No. 9 Craven Gardens, on the Uxbridge Road (later numbered No. 99 Uxbridge Road) in West Ealing, since 1881 and this was to be her home for the next three decades.⁵,⁶ She owned the house.⁷ It had ten rooms and was detached. It was on the south side of the road and was seven houses east from the junction with Culmington Road (possibly the inspiration for the Mrs. Culmington whom a character in *And Then There Were None* refers to). Its last known residents were Harold Oade and Catherine Kennedy in 1953. The house was demolished in the mid-1960s

---

³ Ibid, pp. 62-63.
⁴ Charles Jones, *Ealing: From Village to Corporate Town*, (1901), p. 95.
⁵ Censuses, 1881-1911.
⁶ *Kelly's Directories*, 1887-1914.
⁷ Land Values Book, Ealing South, 1910.

Chapter Two: Mrs. Margaret Miller

and an office block is now on the site. On either side of the house there were many other similar houses, just to the west of the new Broadway where some of Ealing's main shops and the town hall were located.

The house and grounds were described in some detail by Agatha. She wrote, 'Grannie's house and garden had a tremendous fascination for me'.[8]

There were numerous prints on its walls. There was a coloured map of New York City (where Mrs. Miller once lived) on the bathroom wall, 'also an object of interest to me'. In the spare bedroom 'was a set of coloured prints for which I had a deep affection'. One was Winter Sports, showing a man on a sheet of ice, dragging a fish up through a small hole. She thought it was melancholy.[8]

Then there was the Nursery. Agatha divided this into territories. The front part which extended out with a bay window was called the Muriel Room – from the term oriel window. The back part was the Dining Hall, covered as it was by a Brussels carpet. Other floor coverings were allocated by her as different rooms. Apparently she 'moved, busy and important, from one room of my house to another, murmuring under my breath. Nursie (Julie Adams, born in Torquay in 1852, but never identified by name), as peaceful as ever, sat stitching'.[9]

On one occasion Agatha and Julie were wandering on land that belonged to a farmer and he shouted out them 'I'll boil you alive', which impression remained with the little girl for a long time.[10] There were several dairies and a few market gardens in Ealing of the 1890s but few farms, so though we cannot be sure which one this was, but the Drayton Green Farm, run by Frederick and Thomas Cain, might be most likely as the other farms in Ealing were a significant distance to the north and north east of Mrs. Miller's house.

Mrs Miller's bed was another source of fascination. It was an immense four poster mahogany structure, with red damask curtains. It was a feather bed and early in the mornings, the young Agatha would dress and climb in. She was welcomed by her great aunt, who was always awake by six.[11]

In the drawing room downstairs, it was 'crowded with marquetry furniture and Dresden china, and perpetually shrouded in gloom because of the conservatory erected outside'. The room was only used for parties. She described it as 'a wonderful period piece'. There was little room in it to move about, for there were chairs, cabinets, oil lamps and small tables. Though it was cold, Agatha was the only one to use it and that was because it had a piano and because her great aunt bought her musical scores, she used to play them for hours on end. Fortunately the door could be closed so no one else need hear them.[11]

---

[8] Agatha Christie, *An Autobiography*, (1977), p. 39.
[9] Ibid, pp. 39-40.
[10] Janet Morgan, *Agatha Christie: A Biography* (1984), p. 16.
[11] Agatha Christie, *An Autobiography*, (1977), p. 40.

Next to this room was the morning room which she always thought of as sewing room. It transpires that many houses had one and this was where poor relatives would sit and sew. Although well treated by the owner of the house the servants despised them. The sewing these women did was it would seem not very good, but this was excused on the grounds that they had had unfortunate lives. Agatha recalled, 'So, in the morning room, Miss James sat and sewed with patterns all around her, and a sewing machine in front of her'.[11]

The dining room seems to have been the nerve centre of the house. Agatha wrote that it was here where 'Grannie passed her life in Victorian contentment'. The furniture was inevitably mahogany; a central table surrounded by chairs. The windows were thickly draped. Margaret sat either at the table in a huge leather backed chair, where she would write letters or she would sit in a big velvet armchair by the fireplace. There would be books everywhere, on the chairs, the table and the sofa for she bought a great many. Some were meant for other people but she forgot to always send them. She would play verbal games with the young Agatha, one titled 'a chicken from Mr. Whiteley's' in which Agatha would pretend to be the chicken who is trussed up, cooked and then come alive again just before she is carved.[12]

There was also a side cupboard by the side door into the garden and each morning Mrs. Miller would go there. Her great niece would appear, too, and the former would ask, 'Now, what can a little girl want here?' There were rows of jam jars, packets of dried fruits, sacks of sugar, tea and flour and other foodstuffs. The old lady would also account for the food eaten on the previous day so as to avoid wastage.[13]

Then there was the garden. Agatha later wrote, 'In the Ealing garden it is always summer – and particularly hot summer'. She enjoyed the hot dry air and the smell of roses. It was actually a small square of green grass surrounded with standard rose trees, but she saw it as a world. Her great aunt was proud of the roses and attributed their size and beauty to the bedroom slops.[13]

Agatha recalled the Sundays she stayed there (it is not known whether they were church goers; at this time Ealing had one of London's largest number of regular worshippers). This was when her other elderly relations would visit, including her great aunt's sister, Mary, from Bayswater, uncles and others. Harriet (of whom more anon) was Mary's servant and would assist with taking off outdoor shoes and putting more comfortable ones on. Conversation often centred around shops and the quality of goods recently purchased. 'You wouldn't have cared for it Margaret. Not good quality material, very tawny, not at all like that last plum colour velvet'. Sometimes they would bring goods

---

[12] Ibid, p. 40-41.
[13] Ibid, p. 41.

bought from London shops for Mrs. Miller and she would settle the accounts with cash. Commissions for the forthcoming week would also be discussed.[14]

Sunday dinner was a substantial meal. An enormous joint would be served, then cherry tart and cream, a large piece of cheese and then dessert on the Sunday best plates, possibly French china and well decorated. In the centre of each was a fruit. Agatha later used these herself after Mrs. Miller's death. Evidently the fruits were covered up with mats so everyone had to guess what was there and this was 'always a thrilling moment'.[14]

After lunch there was repose. The old ladies would sleep and the men often went out for a walk. Agatha would have the rocking chair. After about an hour or so, they would play a game called Schoolmaster, sitting in a row and asking quiz type questions to each other. They would later take tea and the uncles would leave first.[15]

On weekdays Mrs. Miller's social life revolved around a different set of people. Agatha explained:

> 'Ealing at that time had the same characteristics as Cheltenham or Leamington Spa. The retired military and navy men came in large quantities for the healthy air and the advantage of being so near London. Grannie led a thoroughly social life – she was a sociable woman at all times. Her house was always full of old Colonels and generals for whom she would embroider waistcoats and knit bed socks'.[16]

George Orwell found this Anglo-Indian society to exist in Ealing in the 1920s, too, 'I hadn't known till then that there was a considerable Anglo-Indian colony in Ealing. Talk about discovering a new world', but a writer in the next decade said that only a few remained. In 1900 Mrs. Miller had two neighbours who would have fitted the bill; at No. 91 Major General Thomas Mercer and at No. 105 was Lieutenant Colonel Henry Buchanan. A friend of Mrs. Miller's was Mrs. Barry, who claimed to have survived the 'Black Hole of Calcutta'; Agatha's biographer said this was implausible, but as this atrocity occurred in 1756 and Agatha was born in 1890 and cannot have heard this until a few years after the latter year, it was not improbable but impossible.[17] This story teller was Mrs. Mary Barry, aged 61 and born in Calcutta, was the wife of Major General Charles William Barry of No. 7 Creffield Road in 1901 and late of the Royal Engineers.[18]

---

[14] Ibid, pp. 41-42.
[15] Ibid, p. 44.
[16] Ibid, pp. 44-45.
[17] Janet Morgan, *Agatha Christie: A Biography*, (1984), p. 16.
[18] Census, 1901.

Agatha found these old men rather embarrassing for they made unfunny jokes about what food she was going to eat and they were amused by her answers.[19]

Mrs Miller had servants, of course, as had any middle-class Victorian or Edwardian household. Agatha remembered Hannah Dyson the cook, in particular as 'the pillar of Grandmother's establishment' and she was old and wrinkled, 'a bag of bones with deeply lined face and stooped shoulders. She cooked magnificently'. She made bread three times a week and Agatha was allowed to help and to make her own cottage loaves and twists. The two once fell out when Agatha asked her what giblets were and teased her about them because she was told they were not what well brought up young ladies asked about. Hannah was born in the west riding of Yorkshire in about 1832. She had been employed by Margaret from at least 1871-1901, but probably died a few years later as she was not listed in the 1911 census.[20]

In 1881 there was, as well as Hannah, a housemaid. There were also two servants belonging to Frederick and Clarissa, later Agatha's parents. In 1891, there was also Eliza White, a 26 year old parlour maid from Edinburgh. In 1901 there were three servants; apart from Hannah, there was Ethel Glenfield, a 24 year old parlourmaid cum domestic servant, born in Embleton, Buckinghamshire and Bridget Fenelly, a housemaid from Ireland. In 1911 there were only two; Emily Chilten, a 26 year old house and parlour maid, born in Grimston, Norfolk and Elizabeth Herriard, a 33 year old cook from Caversham, Berkshire.[21]

Servants were commonplace and very necessary for the middle class. Mrs. Miller's neighbours employed them. Next door at the doctor's was a housekeeper and a housemaid. His neighbour, another doctor, lived with his wife and daughter; they had two female servants.[22]

There were registries for servants in Ealing and adverts for servants frequently appeared in the local press. Most lived with their employers but by no means all. Census returns for working class households sometimes list daughters being employed in domestic service. Most servants were unmarried young women because they were cheaper and did those essential household jobs, i.e. cooking and cleaning, but upper-class households would employ some male servants, usually a gardener; in the wealthiest of households there would be indoor male servants, such as those staples of detective fiction, the butler and the valet.

Most interestingly, on census night (2nd April in 1911) there was Agatha Miller, a 20 year old single woman from Torquay, Devon who is not recorded as having any employment.[22] She is also listed as living at her mother's house

---

[19] Agatha Christie, *An Autobiography*, (1977), p. 45.
[20] Ibid, p. 56.
[21] Censuses, 1881-1911.
[22] Census, 1911.

Chapter Two: Mrs. Margaret Miller

in Ashfield as well, probably meaning that Ashfield was her usual residence but that she happened to be one of her extended trips to Ealing at the same time.

Agatha often stayed with her Auntie-Grannie. She was certainly in Ealing in 1895 for she remembered meeting her sister Margaret there when she returned from Paris. She would usually go there with her nurse. Sometime when her parents were in America she might be there for months, as occurred in 1897. In that year her mother wrote to her in Ealing, 'I am sure you are very very happy with dear Grannie. You must be good to her and love her very much'. She certainly seems to have enjoyed going there as she wrote, 'Ashfield was home and accepted as such; Ealing, however, was an excitement. It had all the romance of a foreign country. One of its principal joys was its lavatory. It had a splendidly large mahogany lavatory seat. Sitting on it one felt exactly like a Queen in her throne'.[23]

In a letter written in 1968 the now famous author recalled her great aunt:

'I spent a lot of time as a child, with my Auntie-Granny, who then lived at Ealing, and she used to tell me long stories about her childhood, brought up with the Kelseys of Prinsted, and I also heard about Fanny Clark and the Crowders'.[24]

In her autobiography, Agatha Christie described how she thought up the character she liked most of all, Miss Marple. Apparently she was:

'the sort of old lady who would have been rather like some of my grandmother's Ealing cronies – old ladies whom I have met in so many villages where I have gone to stay as a girl. Miss Marple was not in any way a picture of my grandmother; she was far more fussy and spinsterish than my grandmother ever was. But one thing she did have in common with her – though a cheerful person, she always expected the worst of everyone and everything, and was, with almost frightening accuracy, usually proved right'.[25]

She added, 'I shouldn't be surprised if so and so isn't going on' and despite having no grounds for believing so, she was proved correct. 'A downy fellow, that – I don't trust him'. When the man, a bank clerk, was found to have embezzled money she was unsurprised and nodded her head. 'Yes,' she said, 'I've known one or two like him'. When someone tried to con her out of savings, she remarked, 'I know his kind. I knew what he was after. I think I'll just ask a few friends to tea and mention that young man like that is going round'. There were local newspaper stories and letters about men who called on middle-class households and attempted to persuade the householder to part

---

[23] Agatha Christie, *An Autobiography*, (1977), pp. 53, 38-39.
[24] Letter from Agatha Christie to Mr. Way, 15th June 1968, The Agatha Christie Archive.
[25] Agatha Christie, *An Autobiography*, (1977), p. 435.

with their money for a charity, out of sympathy or on some bogus scheme. Unsurprisingly, 'Grannie's prophecies were much dreaded' and she foretold the sad end of a pet squirrel Agatha's siblings had. It escaped.[26]

Agatha's official biographer also noted another similarity between Miss Marple and Mrs. Miller. In *At Bertram's Hotel*, a 1965 Miss Marple novel, the sleuth is staying at her fondly remembered London hotel and spends some of her time shopping at the Army and Navy Stores in Victoria, which Margaret also enjoyed and the two shared a liking for buying table napkins and bath towels in the sales.[27] Agatha also read *The Adventures of Her Baby* by Mrs. Molesworth written in 1881 whilst in Ealing, which concerns the adventures of a four year old abroad who is lost from their family.[28]

When Mrs. Miller was growing old and increasingly had difficultly seeing things, she, 'as elderly people do, progressively more suspicious of everybody: of her servants, of men who came to mend the pipes, of the piano tuner, and so on'. After all, by 1911 she no longer had the services of aged retainer Hannah Dyson.[29]

In the stories, Miss Marple has a lot to say about trust and human nature. At the end of *Sleeping Murder*, the last of the stories, two young people are admonished by her, 'You trust people. I never have for years'. In *They Do It with Mirrors*, a friend says to Miss Marple, 'nothing has ever surprised you, you always believe the worst', to which she replies, 'The worst is so often true'. She constantly refers to human nature being weak or wicked. In this, of course, she mirrored Mrs. Miller.

Mrs. Miller was a very self-assured and confident old lady. She never doubted herself and came out with a number of dictums:

'Always think the worst about people'.

'Gentlemen need attention and three proper meals a day'.

'Gentlemen like a figure'.

'Gentlemen can be very agreeable, but you can't trust one of them'.

'A husband should never be left alone too long'.

On talking to male friends over tea, 'I hope your wife won't object'.

On talking to a young man who had made a servant pregnant, 'Well, are you going to do the right thing by Harriet?' (this was a reference to Mrs. Miller's sister's servant, whose surname we never know nor whether she was married to her seducer)

---

[26] Ibid, pp. 435-436.
[27] Janet Morgan, *Agatha Christie: A Biography*, (1984), p. 176.
[28] Ibid, p. 18.
[29] Agatha Christie, *An Autobiography*, (1977), p. 245.

Chapter Two: Mrs. Margaret Miller

'Never get into a train with a single man'.

'Waste not want not'.

'Every woman should have fifty pounds in five pound notes in case of emergencies (Agatha later found £5 notes stuffed in her great aunt's belongings)'.

She could also be very perceptive. When an unmarried relation came to her house for lunch with an American clergyman who had health problems, she told the woman, 'May, that man's in love with you'. She denied it, but Mrs. Miller insisted it was so. The two later were very happily married.[30]

She was disappointed in February 1901 when she went up to London to see the funeral procession of Queen Victoria. She had arranged a vantage point but was unable to reach it because of the huge crowds and was very tearful.[31]

---

[30] Ibid, pp. 187.
[31] Ibid, pp. 57-58.

CHAPTER THREE
TRANSPORT IN EALING

One local issue in Ealing which made an impact on Agatha was the radical development in transport at the turn of the twentieth century. One of the many attractions of Ealing was the excellence of its transport links. These made it easy to go to and from London and to reach other destinations further afield.

There was the road network. The principal road which ran through Ealing was the Uxbridge Road, which went from Shepherd's Bush to the east, through Acton, then Ealing, then Hanwell, Southall, Hayes, Hillingdon and Uxbridge. This route had existed since the Middle Ages and had been under the care of the Uxbridge Turnpike trust since 1714. Stage coaches had traversed this road, once known as the Oxford Road, from London to Oxford since the seventeenth century, taking two days, though a horseman could make the journey in a day. Many of these stage coaches also delivered mail and had regular stops to collect and deliver it, as well as passengers, at the coaching inns along the road.

By the middle of the nineteenth century, stage coaches were in decline and ceased entirely by about 1879, due to competition from the new railways and also horse buses. These travelled shorter distances, but carried more passengers and were more frequent. Several served Ealing. Mostly these were small operators with only a few vehicles in their fleets. For example, Mr. Crockford ran three daily services of his horse bus which travelled from Hanwell to Ealing and eventually to Regent's Circus in central London. In fact, the horse bus was probably more convenient for many residents wishing to travel to central London because train travel up to 1863 only went as far as Paddington; there was no railway line from Paddington until 1863 to take a traveller further into London. In the 1890s horse traffic was predominant on the local streets, as a Major Cattley, an Ealing resident, later recalled:

> 'Nearly all the transport was horse-drawn, and the tradesmen delivered goods to their clients by horse drawn conveyances ... Very characteristic of this period were the two-wheeler corporation dust carts, which were used to keep the roads clean ... Horse drawn funerals were constantly seen on the road to the cemetery ... the road became noisy when the trams arrived as well as the horse buses along the Uxbridge Road and the High Street'.[1]

By the 1900s, however, they were being slowly replaced by motor buses which ran along the Uxbridge Road, improving services to passengers still

---

[1] Cited in Jonathan Oates, *Ealing: A Concise History,* (2014), pp. 52-53.

further. One such company was the London General Omnibuses, running motor buses from East Ham through London as far as Ealing from 1911.

By this time the roads were maintained by the Urban District Council of Ealing and principally the department headed by surveyor Charles Jones. He described the upkeep of the roads in his memoirs. In 1901 there were 52 miles of roads in Ealing; three quarters of which were paved, kerbed and channelled. The Uxbridge Road was a wood paved road ('entirely a new experience ... but I have no doubt it will very soon be followed by other districts') about two miles in length.[2]

Railways came locally in 1838. The Great Western Railway was a company formed to take passengers to and from London and Bristol and its chief engineer was I. K. Brunel. The first railway stop outside London Paddington was, until 1868, Ealing Haven, later known as Ealing Broadway. Initially there were only six trains stopping here in either direction each day, but as time went by the frequency increased and prices fell. In 1871 another local station along this line was opened in Ealing, Castlebar and Ealing Dean Halt, eventually known as West Ealing station in 1899, though services here were less frequent than they were at Ealing Broadway. In the early twentieth century there was a loop from West Ealing to Greenford, with a stop at Castlebar Halt.

The other train link to Ealing was the District Railway line, which had stops at Ealing Common, on the eastern part of the parish and at another station just to the north of Ealing Broadway station in July 1879. On another branch of the same line from 1883 were stations at South Ealing and, in 1908, Northfields, continuing eventually to Hounslow. These met with great applause in the local press, but they also stated that they needed to run until later in the night in order to enable Ealing residents to attend theatre performances in London and return home.

Since 1870 there had been schemes afoot for another form of road transport; the trams. At first this was for a horse tram service to run from Shepherd's Bush to Southall, through Acton and Ealing. Trams would be laid on the roads in order to make it possible for horses to pull trams with more passengers than could the horse buses. However, little of the track was built and the company went out of business. Other companies took it on, but it was not until the London United Electric Tramway Company took it over that the scheme became imminent and the plan was for the tram tracks to run from Shepherd's Bush to Uxbridge. Furthermore, since they would be electric powered, tram poles and cabling would need to be erected along the route.

Reactions locally were varied. They were important because the company needed permission from the councils along the route for the laying of the tram tracks on their roads. Some councils were positive about the new system, some needed incentives, but one council was opposed and that was Ealing.

---

[2] Charles Jones, *Ealing: From Village to Corporate Town*, (1901), pp. 31-33.

Chapter Three: Transport in Ealing

The council was supported by some of its inhabitants. They argued that trams would disfigure the streets and lead to a decline in the town's prosperity. Jones was opposed to it. Property values would fall, cheap houses and shops would appear in great numbers. There was also the suggestion that the council run its own tram service.

Others were supportive of the scheme. The tram company paid for seven issues of pro-tram propaganda and pro-tram councillors made speeches linking trams with incorporation and progress. They thought that it would provide cheap, efficient and reliable transport, especially for the working class, for whom trains were expensive and did not provide a useful service. Liberal councillors tended to support the scheme.

Both opponents and proponents argued the case out in the columns of the local newspaper, *The Middlesex County Times*, which in its editorials supported the tram cause.

Eventually the pro-tram councillors grew in number following the local election. The council managed to wring numerous conditions from the tram company, such as the company paying the council's legal bills for their anti-tram stance, paying annual rates as well as an additional £400-500 per annum and allowing the council to use the tram poles as lamp posts, and permission was finally granted in 1899 by nine votes to two. As the trams ran along the Uxbridge Road they would pass by Mrs. Miller's house constantly.

[Postcard image (courtesy of Paul Lang) of a tram on the Uxbridge Road]

Agatha described it thus:

'The trams came to Ealing – and local opinion erupted in fury. A terrible thing to happen to Ealing; such a fine residential neighbourhood, such wide streets, such beautiful houses – to have trams clanging up and down! The word Progress was uttered but howled down. Everyone wrote to the Press, to their M.P., to anyone they could think of to write to. Trams were common – they were noisy – everyone's health would suffer. There was an excellent service of brilliant red buses, with Ealing on them in large letters, which ran from Ealing Broadway to Shepherd's Bush, and another extremely useful bus, though more humble in appearance, which ran from Hanwell to Acton. And there was the good old fashioned Great Western Railway; to say nothing of the District Railway. Trams were simply not needed. But they came, and there was weeping and gnashing of teeth'.

It is thought that this crisis led to the eleven year old Agatha's first item in print, written on the 10th July 1901, the day when the trams began to run, a four verse poem, one of whose verses read as follows:

> 'When first the electric trams did run
> In all their scarlet glory,
> 'Twas well, but ere the day was done,
> It was another story'.

One of her Auntie Grannie's military men friends (possibly Major General Thomas Mercer who resided at No. 91 Uxbridge Road) took the verses to the local newspaper office – not stated whether this was the *Middlesex County Times*, established in 1866 (at No. 61 The Broadway in 1901) or the more recent *Ealing Gazette* (No. 123 Uxbridge Road), to suggest it was published. However, though Agatha later wrote, 'I was elated at seeing myself in print' in her autobiography and all who mention it pass this on as being fact, there is no evidence that it was published locally. A search of both newspapers for 1901 and 1902 does not uncover it.[3] This is a great shame; to have located the first published work of an author who was to become globally renowned would have been a major discovery and nationally newsworthy. Hopefully in the future a sharp-eyed scholar will locate it.

However, as years passed the trams became more acceptable. They ran every three minutes and by 1904 the route was extended as far as Uxbridge. Dr. Patten, the medical officer of health, wrote, 'as a resident of the main road, and after several months experience, that if only the serious noise occasioned by them could be modified, there is little but good to be said of them'. The tramway was opened with great ceremony on the 10th June 1901; even opponents turned out to celebrate the fact.[4]

---

[3] Agatha Christie, *An Autobiography*, (1977), p. 127.
[4] *Ealing Medical Officer of Health Annual Report* (1901), cited in Jonathan Oates, *Ealing: A Concise History, (2014)*, p. 53.

Chapter Three: Transport in Ealing

The other form of transport seen in Ealing at this time was the car. The first one seen in Ealing was in 1896 when John Sanders, owner of one of Ealing's leading department stores owned one and advertised giving paying passengers short rides in it. Mr. Ravenshaw had a car in 1898 and gave a talk to a local society.

The maximum speed was about 18 m.p.h. but in the next decade the county council reduced it to 5 m.p.h.

CHAPTER FOUR
SOCIAL LIFE IN EALING

There were a large number of clubs and societies of all types in Edwardian Ealing as well as places of entertainment. Sporting clubs abounded; especially those for playing tennis and cricket. Some middle-class families had tennis matches on their lawns; as recalled by Christmas Humphreys at his parents' house on Montpelier Road prior to 1914. There was also the Ealing Ladies' Badminton and Hockey Club founded in about 1888. The Ealing Natural History Club was one of many less physical clubs.

Agatha was enrolled in a dancing school in Ealing (as well as one in Torquay), of which there then were many, when she was aged about nine 'and very shy'. There were many boys in the class and on being asked to dance the Lancers with one who was a year or two her senior, she declined citing being unable to dance, but eventually danced with one William 'my first love', whom she never saw again. Mrs. Wordsworth was in charge. Miss Hickey tried to teach her the waltz, but without much success though she thought it would be the only dance that it would be useful to know. Unfortunately it seems difficult to trace the school; none of the individuals mentioned are listed in the 1901 Ealing census and nor is Mrs. Wordsworth's school advertised in the local press. The 1900-1901 directory for Ealing does not mention any householder with the surname Wordsworth so her identity remains a mystery.[1]

More sedentary, Agatha enjoyed the theatre. According to *Ealing Illustrated*, 'as is natural in so cultured a community things dramatic arouse much interest and attention'. This took the form of amateur dramatics and also professional for 'there are few weeks during the season that announcements of some high-class dramatic entertainment are not to be seen'. This was principally at the Lyric Theatre in the east end of Ealing Broadway, where the D'Oyley Carte and other companies had performed. The Lyric was 'one of the cosiest and best appointed places of theatrical entertainment'. It also boasted a ballroom and a lounge. It was well furnished and smart inside.[2]

After seeing Sir Henry Irving in *Becket* at Exeter, her great aunt took her to the theatre. Assuming that this was in Ealing, it would have been the Lyric Theatre until 1899 when it was replaced by the Ealing Theatre, later renamed the Ealing Hippodrome when it became largely a music hall not a theatre. This was on the north side of Ealing Broadway. They went once or twice a week, mainly to musical comedies.

---

[1] Agatha Christie, *An Autobiography*, (1977), p. 101.
[2] Anon, *Ealing Illustrated*, (1893), pp. 15-16.

By the 1900s cinema began to be established in Ealing. There was in 1912 the Theatre Charming in West Ealing. Along Northfields Avenue there were two; at the north end was the West Ealing Kinema and at the south end was Northfields Cinema in 1913. In central Ealing the theatre was replaced by the Hippodrome Cinema and a skating rink on Bond Street became the Walpole Picture Palace in 1912. But by then theatre goers could go to central London with the improved transport then available.

Finally we should not forget Ealing Film Studios. Although it is often stated that it was established on Ealing Green in 1902, indeed, the board outside the studios proclaims this as a fact, it was not actually until later that decade that William Barker did so. He bought West Lodge on the Green with three acres behind it in 1908. It has been suggested that lighting to the west of London was better than it was in the east and so this could have been why he looked at Ealing. By 1912 it was claimed to be the largest film studios in England. Whether Agatha was aware of it is another question, for a local newspaper reporter in that year noted 'for nearly three years past, the workshop of this, the largest national business in national business in motion photography, should have been lying hidden amongst our midst'. Many local craftsmen were employed in making props and open spaces in Ealing were used for filming, such as Ealing Common in Barker's reverent film about Queen Victoria. He also adapted books and plays, using well known theatre actors to do so.

Mrs. Miller's influence on the young writer came in another way. She asked Agatha to read to her reported murder cases and trials from the 1890s and 1900s.[3] These included some well-known cases, not only the celebrated case of Dr. Crippen in 1910 but also Seddon the poisoner in 1912. At this time, the national and local press devoted columns to such cases and trials were covered in great detail of a type never seen before nor since. They were not verbatim, but were lengthy. Speeches of barristers, judge, witnesses being examined and then cross examined, and so on, it was all there, and could carry over several issues of daily newspapers. *The Middlesex County Times* was Ealing's first weekly newspaper, and as with most newspapers at the time, had adverts on the front page. Inside were very detailed accounts of council meetings, sports matches, meetings of clubs and societies, church and political news as well as inquests, obituaries and notices of births, marriages and deaths. The seamier side of life was not neglected wither, so reports of crime and poverty were included. It did not just cover Ealing but places nearby, such as Hanwell, Acton, Hammersmith, Brentford and Kew. As with most local newspapers, it also featured national and international news and serialised fiction. The letters page allowed local complaints to be aired (often about the activities of the council) as well as readers to debate key local topics over numerous issues. *The Ealing Gazette* had become the town's second newspaper and tended to be less formal

---

[3] Agatha Christie, *An Autobiography*, (1977), p. 244.

and livelier. It is possible the young Agatha read her about such Ealing murders as that of Anne Covell by Alfred Perry of 1910, which took place at No. 1 Florence Terrace and that of Arthur Benbow who shot and killed his landlady two years later, which are both detailed later.

CHAPTER FIVE
DEATHS IN THE FAMILY

Death became rather closer to home to Agatha. Frederick Alvah Miller, Agatha's father, born in 1846, died in Ealing on the 26th November 1901 and was buried in Ealing cemetery three days later. Apparently he was staying at his stepmother's house because he was looking for work; not easy for a middle aged man with no special training or experience of paid work. He became ill and his wife and two daughters came to Ealing to be with him. Agatha was 'unhappy and frightened, praying earnestly that father night get well again'. She did not attend the funeral, being a child, and so 'I wandered about the house in a queer state of turmoil'. He was buried in Ealing cemetery, on the east side of South Ealing Road. Regrettably there is no report of his death and funeral in the local newspaper and he does not appear to have left a will. It was rare for the local press to report deaths on non-residents.[1]

[Grave of Agatha's parents and Auntie-Grannie, Ealing Cemetery (image © Dr. Jonathan Oates)]

---

[1] Agatha Christie, *An Autobiography*, (1977), pp. 110-113.

The wording on the grave ran as follows:

> In Loving Remembrance of
> FREDERICK ALVAH MILLER
> OF NEW YORK AND TORQUAY
> WHO DIED 26TH NOVEMBER 1901 AGED 55
> WHAT DO THOU KNOWEST NOT NOW
> BUT THOU SHALL KNOWEST THEREAFTER

His widow purchased, from Ealing Council's Burial Board, for the sum of £4 4s., plot No. 12G in the E portion of consecrated ground at the cemetery on the 3rd December 1901. On the 5th November 1905, she bought the adjacent plot, No. 13G, for the same price.[2] After her husband's funeral, she took some leaves from a Beech tree from the cemetery and kept them with the funeral order of service.[3]

By 1914 Mrs Miller was growing old. Agatha recalled that 'she had become very blind indeed with cataract, and she was, of course, too old to be operated on'. However, she was sensible enough to realise that, though it would be very hard leaving her Ealing home and all her friends behind, she could hardly live alone and that servants were unlikely to stay. Yet she wept as her life was unearthed around her – she had lived in the same house for over 30 years. She could not bear to part with most of her possessions, so these had to be transported down to Devon. They included a moth-eaten velvet dress, lengths of silk from the Army and Navy Stores, prints for servants' dresses, a clothes basket full of flour, homemade liqueur, packets of sugar and butter, letters and papers, and an old envelope full of £5 notes.[4]

At the Millers' Torquay home, Ashfield, during the First World War, she worried about Agatha, who was working in a hospital for men wounded in the war. She was concerned that her great niece would come to harm, declaring that such work was 'Not at all suitable you ought to have someone to come down and meet you and chaperone you', to which the young woman replied, 'Well, they can't spare anyone to do things like that'.[5] She died at Ashfield on the 29th May 1919, aged 90. When her will was proved on the 19th July 1919, her estate was worth £7,280 2s. 4d. gross and £7,222 14s. 10d. net. Her will had been made on the 18th February 1910 and the executors were James Watts and William Bayley; only the former was alive when it was proved. Her great nieces Margaret and Agatha were left £1,000 each; her great nephew only £500,

---

[2] Funeral papers, 1901 & 1905, The Agatha Christie Archive.
[3] Janet Morgan, *Agatha Christie: A Biography,* (1984), p. 33.
[4] Ibid, pp. 242-245.
[5] Ibid, p. 241.

Chapter Five: Deaths in the Family

the same that her sister Florence was left. The executors were allocated £10 each and apart from three other small sums, her niece received the residue.[6]

On the 4th June 1919 Margaret Miller was buried in the same grave plot as Frederick Miller in Ealing Cemetery (the same cemetery and in the same year as was Grace Stevenson, a black servant who had committed suicide by gas after marital disappointment, grief from her family and racial taunts by errand boys – the story made minor local headlines, 'Coloured Woman's Lament'). The wording on another side of the same grave was thus:

> Also of
> MARGARET MILLER
> DIED 29TH MAY 1919 IN HER NINETY FIRST YEAR
> TRUST IN THE MERCY OF GOD FOREVER AND EVER
> PSALM 52 V8

On the 5th April 1926 Agatha's mother, Clarissa, died at her elder daughter's house in Cheshire, leaving £16,878 and was also buried in the same plot; on the 9th April. Thus on another side of the same grave as her husband and aunt were the words:

> Also of
> CLARISSA MARGARET MILLER (WIFE OF FREDERICK ALVAH MILLER)
> WHO DIED 5TH APRIL 1926 AGED 72 YEARS
> I BELIEVE IN THE HOLY GHOST, THE LORD AND THE GIVER OF LIFE
> HER CHILDREN RISE UP AND CALL HER BLESSED,
> HER HUSBAND ALSO, AND HE PRAISETH HER

It is presumed that Agatha attended the two latter ceremonies which were all low key and not reported locally. Her husband did not attend his mother-in-law's funeral for he was then abroad on business. There is a notice board at the cemetery's entrance listing four famous people buried there and Agatha's parents make up two of these; regrettably the board does not give their years of birth and misnames Clarissa 'Margaret', yet it usefully shows where the graves are.

None of these three would know that Agatha would become a world famous author; her father and great aunt never saw even one of her books in print, though her mother had the pleasure of seeing her daughter having six books published in 1920-1925. It was only after her death and with the publication of *The Murder of Roger Ackroyd* later that year that her reputation became assured.

---

[6] Will of Margaret Miller.

It is well known that Agatha disappeared for eleven days in December 1926. On the front page of Ealing's newspaper there was a short and somewhat misleading article on this topic:

> **The Christie Mystery**
>
> Mrs Agatha Christie, the missing novelist, has a brother and sister living in Ealing and much sympathy has been expressed with them in the anxiety they are suffering. Until four years ago Colonel and Mrs. Christie lived at West Kensington and they were frequent visitors to Ealing'.[7]

However, neither of her relatives lived in Ealing; Margaret Watts lived in Cheshire and Louis Monty Miller lived abroad.

[Margaret Watts' gravestone, Ealing Cemetery
(image © Dr. Jonathan Oates)]

However, on the 22nd November 1950, Margaret Frary Watts (known as 'Punkie'), was buried in the same cemetery on a patch next to the that of her parents and great aunt, which had clearly been reserved in 1901. She was

---

[7] *Middlesex County Times*, 11th December 1926.

Chapter Five: Deaths in the Family

Agatha's older sister by 11 years and had married James Watts, a businessman, in 1902.

The wording on her gravestone was as follows:

> MARGARET FRARY
> BELOVED WIFE OF JAMES WATTS
> OF ABNEY HALL, CHEADLE, CHESHIRE
> AND DAUGHTER OF CLARISSA AND FREDERICK ALVAH MILLER
> IN HAPPINESS AND GRACE, OCT 23RD 1950
> AGED 71 YEARS.

Their brother Louis, who died in France in 1929 was buried there but not in the same grave as his parents and elder sister. Presumably the burial of her sister was a quiet ceremony such as the others had had and went unreported despite Agatha's international fame by now. The Ealing of 1950 was a rather different Ealing of the pre-1914 years or even 1926, with a far larger population and a far more socially diverse one in class terms. There was even a Labour M.P. (James Hudson) as well as a Conservative one as the place was split into two constituencies. That said, there were still numerous private schools and many of the Edwardian era department stores were still there.

CHAPTER SIX
CRIME IN FACT AND FICTION

Ealing was not a suburb that was known for crime. However, there were three murders which occurred there during the years 1890-1914 and the latter two were ones that the young Agatha would certainly have been aware of. None of the three, however, presented any mystery whatsoever and two of these were from the working-class milieu.

There had also been a grim discovery in a house next door to the Original Old Hats pub on the Uxbridge Road in West Ealing on the morning of the 3rd October 1893. James Benjamin Scotcher, a general and horse dealer, aged 52 and born in King's Lynn, Norfolk, lived there with his daughter Annie aged seven and born in Ealing, and his niece, Agnes Moorby, aged 29, born in Hampton Wick, Surrey and a domestic assistant. However, on that day there was 'a crime which is happily without a parallel in this modern suburb'. That morning Scotcher wanted bacon for breakfast so Agnes left the house to buy some in a nearby shop but on her return found the door locked. Summoning help, they were horrified to find the bodies of Scotcher and his daughter, both dead. Annie had had her head cut off with razor blows and her father had also had his throat cut, the bloodstained razor in his hand.[1]

It was no great feat of detection for the police to state that Scotcher had killed his daughter and then committed suicide, after having read his last letter, that he was unable to live after being unable to pay his creditors and so it was best that he and his daughter were no longer alive. Yet that was not all, as the newspaper noted, there was a revelation that was 'repulsive in the story of depravity it brings to light'. Scotcher had arrived with his wife in West Ealing in the 1870s. Agnes, the daughter of his wife's family, came with them. In 1885 when she was in hospital, Scotcher seduced his niece and she bore him a daughter, who bore his surname. The four lived together but Scotcher's wife died shortly afterwards and the three then lived together. It is not known if Scotcher's wife was aware of the identity of the father of the child, but the decision was clearly taken to pass her off as their own to save Agnes' reputation.[1]

The next murder was arguably closer to home, seventeen years later. George Henry Perry, born in 1883 to respectable parents in Essex, had served in the Royal Garrison Artillery from 1900-1907 in Aden and in India, being discharged with a good character, and shortly after his discharge he went to

---
[1] *Middlesex County Times*, 7th October 1893.

Ealing. Here he met Annie Covell, born in Ealing in 1882, a self-employed dressmaker, the youngest daughter to Edward Covell, a retired policeman, now working as a caretaker, and Mary Ann, his wife. The two had written to each other previously. They became engaged. He had a job as a window cleaner and lived with her family at No. 1 Florence Terrace (their home since at least 1901) until September 1909, but he paid no rent.[2]

[The house on the right was the scene of the Ealing murder of 1910 (image © Dr. Jonathan Oates)]

On Saturday the 8th January 1910 Annie was invited to a wedding at Hanwell, where she had once lived, where she was a bridesmaid. Perry had not been invited and he became angry. He quarrelled with Annie about this, which was

---

[2] *The Proceedings of the Old Bailey*, www.oldbaileyonline.org.

rare for he was usually very calm and collected. He also threatened to kill her father, by bashing his brains out. Covell told Perry to leave, which he did. Afterwards, Perry went to a shop in Ealing and bought a bread knife and platter; the latter was thrown away on Haven Green.[2]

Two days later, on Monday 10th January he was in the breakfast room of his fiancee's house, where his prospective father-in-law was also present. Annie went upstairs and Perry followed her. Then her mother heard a scream and she went upstairs to investigate. She saw Perry with a bread knife, having cut Annie's throat and now was stabbing her. Perry then walked out of the house as cool as anything. Albert Reece, a page boy in the house, went out for the police and P.C. Robert Drew was found and Reece pointed out Perry to him. He was walking in the direction of the police station.[2]

He was soon arrested and admitted his guilt to Drew, saying 'I am going to give myself up for stabbing a young girl to death at No. 1 Florence Terrace; I went to the house this morning; they started on me, it was no good being sorry for what one has done. I think I have made a job of it'. They went to the police station, where he was charged and made no reply. Meanwhile, Dr. George Herbert Bennett came to the scene and pronounced her dead from the wounds, quite probably inflicted by a knife.[2]

Detective Inspector Edward Barrett accompanied Perry to the magistrates' court and he told the detective, 'If they had let me go when I wanted to this would not have happened; she was invited to a wedding at Hanwell on Saturday as bridesmaid, but they did not invite me; we had a few words over it; when I went into the house at seven o'clock last night, nobody spoke to me; I afterwards returned at 11 and slept in a chair, this morning she was in the breakfast room and I had the knife in my hand and did it, I suppose I had to do it; I could not stop myself'. At the court hearing he told the magistrate, 'I did it and am satisfied'.[2]

He could produce no motive, saying 'I had to do it. I could not stop myself'. At the trial on the 8th February at the Old Bailey before Justice Coleridge, there was some discussion as to whether he was suffering from insanity and had been seized by an uncontrollable desire to kill. Dr. Bennett was asked whether the accused man had any recollection of what he had done, and whether there was an uncontrollable destructive impulse within him. However, the opinion was that he was sane. Perry said 'I am sorry to say that I have done it, I do not think it is much use my saying anything'. This was dismissed and he was found guilty and later hanged at Pentonville Prison on the 1st March 1910 by Henry Pierrepoint. The Covells and their remaining daughter continued to live in their 9 room house where murder had been done.[2]

Although the name Florence Terrace no longer exists, an examination of the electoral registers for 1939 and 1945 shows that this is because it was incorporated into the Mall in the early 1940s and so No. 1 Florence Terrace is now No. 39 The Mall. This was often the fate of small terraces, although in most cases they were amalgamated with neighbouring and larger cousins far earlier in the century.

The last of these concerns one Arthur James Benbow, born in 1860 in Cowley, Middlesex and baptised on the 20th January at St. John's church, Hillingdon. His parents were John, a master mealman and employer of labour, and Adele, his wife, and he had an elder brother and later two younger siblings. The family employed three servants in 1861 and two in 1871. He was still living at home in 1881 and was then still described as being a scholar, but by 1891 was employed as a civil engineer, still resident with his parents, as he was in 1901, though by now they were living in a house on Common Road, Uxbridge. The death of his father in 1908 meant that Benbow had to make his own domestic arrangements, and he moved to Ealing, lodging at various addresses. By 1911 he lived in a two room flat at No. 8 Sunnyside Road, Ealing. No longer in any form of employment, he was a man with a private income, presumably derived from his father's will and any savings he had accrued, and thus did not have to work.[3]

Benbow was described as being 'a perfect gentleman'. Physically he was 'of slight build, and with the stoop of the student, he is of dark sullen features, has a dark moustache, wears spectacles, and usually, a trilby hat'. He had a number of innocent diversions; visiting the Natural History Museum, walking about West Ealing and reading books, chiefly on natural history. However, he had no close friends of either sex, had never married and had not put down roots anywhere.[4]

He also was rather eccentric. He left No. 8 Sunnyside Road in about May 1911 and boarded at a house in Kingsley Avenue, West Ealing, 'one of Ealing's most quiet and residential districts', for about ten months. There had not once spoken to the landlady's five year old child, always spent an hour in the bath and never let anyone see the contents of his large trunks and boxes in which were all his worldly possessions. He was also a hypochondriac, obsessed that he was ill despite doctors telling him that he was not and that an alleged serious illness was but indigestion. He also accused one of his landladies as trying to poison him and reported this to a doctor but had to withdraw his statement when he faced a prosecution for libel.[4]

Leaving this house without giving any prior notice, he briefly stayed in one in Hastings Road. His behaviour there also was remarked upon. He was seen wandering about the house in the early hours of the morning on two occasions. Once he demanded that he needed a doctor immediately on the other he asked that a fish in the pantry be removed because it was unfit to eat. He later profusely apologised.[4]

---

[3] Census returns, 1861-1911.
[4] *Middlesex County Times*, 6th April 1912.

Chapter Six: Crime in Fact and Fiction

On the 13th March 1912 he arrived at No. 5 Kingsley Avenue. There lived Sophia and Sarah Baker, sisters who had been born in Marlborough in 1856 and 1852 respectively. They had formerly traded as dressmakers from the 1890s but had now retired from business at No. 2a Portman Street in Marylebone, London, with two assistants and a servant, and had a private income of their own, but were clearly not very wealthy as they did not have any live in servants and took in a lodger.[4]

Benbow's odd behaviour soon reared its head. Sarah found him trying the front door at six in the morning. He was fully dressed. He said he was ill but when she suggested calling a doctor he refused. Eventually they asked him to leave and he took this most placidly.[4]

Matters came to a head on the 2nd April. Sarah left home at nine to do some shopping and reminded Benbow, before she left, that she wanted him to leave. He went out for a walk an hour later, retuned and read a newspaper. Sophia asked if he wanted breakfast and he said no. He then went into the kitchen and saw Sophia making a pudding. He explained what happened next:

> 'When I went to sleep I had terrible dreams. I thought someone came in and threw something over my head. I thought someone was attending me and was operating upon me. It may have been a delusion on my part. I asked her who had performed an operation on me a fortnight ago in the night and she knew nothing about it'.[4]

On saying that Benbow drew a Colt revolver on her and asked again but the terrified woman was still unable to answer the unanswerable. He fired at point blank range and thus could not miss. The bullet went into her heart and she died instantly. The shocked Benbow drank a little brandy and tried to revive his victim with water. When this failed, he did not know what to do so awaited the return of Sarah. Meanwhile he reloaded his gun in case the neighbours tried to lynch him.[4]

It was a quarter to one that Sarah returned and made the grim discovery. At first she thought her sister had only fainted as she could not see the fatal wound. She dashed out of the house to find help. Benbow said and did nothing. Fortunately a passerby knew that a Dr. George Phillips was attending a patient in the nearby St. Stephen's Road, so he came to No. 5. Benbow was merely sitting on the floor of a ground floor room. The doctor sent his driver for the police.[4]

Benbow tried to leave but the doctor restrained him until two constables arrived. Senior officers came later. Benbow explained 'I am sorry this has happened. I did not mean to shoot her. I meant to frighten her'. He told them of his conversation prior to the shooting. He told them where the gun was but it was not where he claimed. It was eventually found on his person. There was then nearly another fatality when Inspector Deeks examined it and it went off in his hand, nearly missing D.C. Dobbs' head.[4]

When Benbow's room was examined there was found bullets for his revolver in a tin box under his bed. There were also prescriptions, medicines and tablets. In a trunk were four £1 notes, which Benbow asked to be given to him. At the police station he was officially charged with murder and he said 'I object to wilful murder. I did not know it was loaded'.[4]

Next morning he appeared before the magistrates' court in Brentford, where he was remanded in custody for a week. He made another statement 'I didn't explain very well. I am so confused just now that I can't give you a proper idea of what the delusion was. I ought to have had expert advice upon it. I have seen a man up town about it. It sounds very mad. It looks like a case for Broadmoor'.[4]

Meanwhile on the 4th April there was the inquest, held at Ealing Town Hall, presided over by Reginald Kemp, deputy county coroner. Sarah gave her evidence about the identity of the corpse and about finding it. She was questioned about Benbow's mental state, but she said that they had considered him harmless. One juryman put so aggressive questions to the poor lady that he had to leave court. Dr. Phillips was commended on his bravery for remaining in the house with the murderer. Finally the jury had to come to a decision. Was this a case of accidental death, of manslaughter or murder? Given that Benbow had fired at point blank range they deemed it to be the latter, but added that he was of unsound mind. Two days later Sophia was buried in Marlborough and her sister left Ealing.[4]

The proceedings at the magistrates' court continued. Evidence and witnesses were called as they had at the inquest. Dr. Bennett, the police surgeon, stated that Benbow was of unsound mind, believing that he had been operated on without his consent. He did not seem to understand how serious his crime was. However, he was committed for trial at the Old Bailey.[4]

On the 24th April he stood trial, but such was his mental state that Justice Coleridge halted it and deemed him guilty of murder but insane. He was sent to Broadmoor where he died in 1946, aged 86. None of these crimes needed any detective work as they require in Agatha Christie's fiction. Benbow was probably suffering from paranoid schizophrenia, imagining things which were not real. Or as a recent crime historian wrote, he was 'the Ealing weirdo'.[5]

As for the forces of law and order, three names should be mentioned. Chief Inspector Walter Dew, who famously arrested Dr. Crippen in 1910 and was involved as a young policeman in the unsuccessful hunt for 'Jack the Ripper' in 1888, retired to live in Perivale in 1911, which is just to the north of Ealing. More significantly, Sir Travers Humphreys (1867-1956) lived in the 1900s-1940s in Ealing, firstly on Montpelier Road and then at No. 47 Castlebar Road.

---

[5] *Middlesex County Times*, 27th April 1912.

Chapter Six: Crime in Fact and Fiction

He was a barrister, who was a junior prosecutor in the 'Brides in the Bath' murder case in 1915 and as a judge dealt with equally famous trials, the last being that of John George Haigh, the acid bath murderer, in 1949. His second son, Christmas, was equally prominent as a barrister (and writer of detective stories on a small scale). He led the prosecution case against Timothy Evans and Donald Hume, both in 1950, and Ruth Ellis, in 1955, before going on to become a judge. Both lived in the Ealing known to Agatha.

Ealing, as part of the Metropolitan district, had a police presence since 1839, which was at first unpopular because it meant that the ratepayers having higher bills to pay for them. The police station was located on the east side of the High Street and initially there was a sergeant and a few men there, but by Agatha's time the establishment had increased and there was an inspector in charge.

There was no magistrates' court in Ealing until 1919, when one was built on Green Man Lane, West Ealing. Criminal cases were dealt with at Brentford Magistrates' court; sufficiently serious ones would be eventually heard at the Old Bailey.

Ealing and its environs are referred to in a number of Agatha Christie stories, far more than would be expected of the average London suburb and this clearly reflects her experiences there.

[Postcard image (courtesy of Paul Lang) of Haven Green]

Firstly, there is *The Adventure of Hunter's Lodge* in *Poirot Investigates*, a collection of short stories published in 1924. A baronet is murdered in the said house in Derbyshire and the murder weapon is a revolver. The alleged gun is found wrapped in a parcel in the railings then on the centre of Haven Green, Ealing (where in real life Perry had thrown away the platter that he had bought with the knife in 1910), by a 'City gentleman' and handed to the local police, presumably at the police station on the High Street. Haven Green is a small open space just by the Ealing Broadway stations, former manorial land administered by Ealing Council since 1881, and those travelling to work in London from the more prosperous part of Ealing would certainly cross it. It transpires that the gun was a red herring put there by the killer's accomplice (the real gun being disposed of after the shooting) who was in his London club on the day of the shooting and took a District line train to Ealing which Poirot says would only take 20 minutes.

In *The Secret of Chimneys*, a 1925 novel, Anthony Cade is looking for a woman, presumably married, with the surname Revel. He checks a telephone directory and finds that there are six Revels there. One is 'Miss Mary Revel with an address in Ealing'. This is not who he is looking for so she is dismissed from the story therewith, along with a firm of saddlers called Revel, as well.

[Postcard image (courtesy of Paul Lang) of 'Hanwell' Asylum]

Chapter Six: Crime in Fact and Fiction

Hanwell, which is adjacent to the western border of Ealing, appears in the less than wonderful attempt at a thriller, *The Big Four* of 1927. An MI6 agent turns up in Poirot's flat, exhausted and unable to give much information about the mysterious secret criminal organisation known as the Big Four. Poirot and Hastings are decoyed out of the flat and when they return they find the man dead, apparently of natural causes. Then their landlady tells them of a visitor, 'There's a man here from 'Anwell – from the 'Sylum. Did you ever?'

This is a reference to the London County Council Mental Hospital which is in Southall but was often referred to as located in Hanwell because that was the nearest built up settlement when it was built in the early nineteenth century and the name stuck. The characters in the story often refer to it as 'a lunatic asylum', this terminology being rather antique.

The establishment was Middlesex's first public asylum, built in 1829-1831 but which expanded throughout the nineteenth century. It was intended for London's pauper insane, for there were many private asylums in or near London for families who could pay the fees. The first superintendent there was Dr. William Ellis, from 1831-1838, who took the step in enabling the inmates to take part in farming work as therapy, even to the extent of them using potentially lethal implements. Dr. John Conolly, superintendent from 1839-1844 and visiting physician thereafter, had all inmates released from all physical restraints which had never been done on this scale in Britain previously. Conolly also had a private asylum in his house, the Lawns, in nearby Hanwell, until his death in 1866. He was a friend of Sir William Gull, a notable royal physician.

The asylum was enlarged in later decades and its population grew. A chapel was built in the grounds as well as additional accommodation. In many ways it resembled a self-contained village, with supplies coming and going from the adjacent canal. In 1889 its administration was transferred from the Middlesex J.P.s to the newly formed London County Council and by 1937 it was renamed the St. Bernard's Hospital. However, some residents nearby did not like its presence and argued that it inhibited the development of Hanwell, to the extent that there was a movement to rename the place in order to disassociate it with the asylum.

The man is shown up; 'a big burly man in uniform'. He is clearly an attendant at the said hospital, though he is initially referred to as being 'a keeper', but later the more correct 'attendant'. He explains that he is there in pursuit of 'one of my birds ... Escaped last night he did'. When Poirot tells him that he is dead, he 'looked more relieved than otherwise' and adds, 'Well, I daresay it's best for all parties'. They ask if he was dangerous, 'Omicidal, d'you mean? Oh, no. 'armless enough. Persecution mania very acute'. Poirot asks how long has he 'been shut up' and he's told two years.

Might he have been sane, Poirot asks. The 'keeper' replies, 'If he was sane, what would he be doing in a lunatic asylum? They all say they're sane, you know'. They show him the corpse and he identifies him, 'That's him – right enough. Funny sort of bloke, ain't he? Well, gentlemen, I had best go off now and make arrangements under the circumstances. We won't trouble you with the corpse much longer. If there's an hinquest, you will have to appear at it, I daresay'. He is referred to as being callous and uncouth.

The man leaves and Inspector Japp arrives. Poirot realises that the dead man has been poisoned. He then goes to the telephone and asks 'for Hanwell'. 'You are the asylum, yes? I understand there has been an escape today? What is that you say?' It turns out that there has been no escape – though it is worth noting that the man told them that he had escaped last night not today as Poirot later says. As might be expected, the 'keeper' was in fact the murderer, come to see that his job was successful and to meet his principal enemy, Hercule Poirot.

Now, this is not one of Agatha Christie's best books (her husband had recently left her for another woman and she herself disappeared for 11 days) and Poirot is clearly not at his most brilliant. This episode shows him as being rather dense, though no one else is any better. Firstly he allows himself to be not only decoyed away from his principal witness but leaves the man entirely alone and unguarded; and he is killed. Second, the comments of the working-class 'keeper' should have given him away and thus allowed him to be apprehended straight away. Of course there will have to be an inquest – any genuine asylum employee would have known that as the man did not die an expected death in hospital and secondly there is no doubt that Poirot and Hastings would have to attend it as they were the last to see the dead man. As it turns out Poirot does not attend. Finally, as already noted Poirot cannot even remember when the man was alleged to have escaped even though he's been told when a few minutes previously.

Ealing is also referred to in the 1940 novel *One Two Buckle My Shoe*. Whilst investigating the mysterious shooting of his dentist, Poirot visits a Mr. Barnes, apparently a retired civil servant who is resident in No. 88 Castlegardens Road, Ealing. Although there is no street of this name there is a Castlebar Road and Castlebar Park and Castlebar Hill; clearly Agatha has these in mind. Since Castlebar Road is nearest to Ealing Broadway underground station, this is probably meant to be Castlegardens Road. This would certainly be an appropriate place for a wealthy individual to live in, given the number of detached houses which still existed there prior to the 1950s. It takes Poirot five minutes to walk from 'the underground station at Ealing Broadway'. Apparently 'It was a small semi-detached house, and the neatness of the front garden drew an admiring nod from Hercule Poirot'. Barnes has a servant to usher Poirot to the dining room to meet him. On another occasion Poirot finds Mr. Barnes working in his garden. Barnes turns out to have been involved in espionage under the name Albert Chapman and he took an interest in the case because a woman involved in it was a Mrs. Albert Chapman (who is no relation).

Chapter Six: Crime in Fact and Fiction

In *4.50 from Paddington*, a 1950s Miss Marple story, Miss Marple's friend Elspeth MacGillicuddy witnesses a murder on a passing train whilst she is travelling westwards from London, from Paddington – hence the book's title. The police and railway authorities are unable to help. Miss Marple, naturally, takes over the case. The main problem with this train murder is that no body can be found and so has presumably been removed from the train by the killer.

Miss Marple takes the slower 4.33 train from Paddington. Two stops are Haling Broadway and Barwell Heath, which we may assume are corruptions of Ealing Broadway and Hanwell. She leans out of the window at the first station and sees 'A small number of third-class passengers got in at Haling Broadway'. At Barwell Heath several third-class passengers depart. It seems rather unrepresentative of Ealing Broadway that only third-class passengers alight and though Miss Marple later states that due to high taxes only businessmen with expense accounts can travel first-class, one would have thought that some Ealing residents might have been able to afford second-class travel at least.

Although Ealing is not mentioned in the 1944 novel *Towards Zero*, it is possible that a plot device from that book has its roots in a real murder which took place in Ealing in 1936. In that year a tennis coach called Linford Derrick confessed to having bludgeoned his alleged friend, Arthur Wheeler to death in his house in Winscombe Crescent in the Brentham estate. He was lucky to be found only guilty of manslaughter and served a prison sentence. Derrick had been to public school, served as an army officer in the First World War and apparently was the 'right sort' for middle-class circles in Ealing as well as the world of Agatha Christie, though he was also something of a ladies' man. In the novel there is a character called Neville Strange, a tennis player who is handsome and charming. He turns out to be a psychopathic murderer and it is possible that the inspiration was drawn from the Ealing murder – a case that was reported nationally so Agatha almost certainly knew of it. Another Ealing murder with Agatha Christie overtones has to be that of Mrs. Chesney and her mother, killed at No. 22 Montpelier Road in 1954 and where the obvious suspect – the adulterous and poverty stricken ex-naval officer and former public schoolboy Ronald Chesney – appeared to have a perfect alibi as he was apparently not even in the country when the murders occurred, and he stood to benefit financially from his wife's death. On investigation, however, the alibi was found to have been faked.[6,7]

It is also worth mentioning that David Suchet who played Hercule Poirot on television from 1989-2014 and is said to be the definitive interpretation, lived locally for many years. He lived at Bullsbridge Wharf, Southall in 1976-1977, in Broomfield Cottage, Broomfield Place, West Ealing from 1978-1980 and then at No. 28 Creswick Road, Acton, from 1981-1986 (in the 1930s Muriel

---

[6] Jonathan Oates, *Foul Deeds and Suspicious Deaths in Ealing*, (2006), pp. 158-163.
[7] Jonathan Oates, *Ronald Chesney: The Middle Class Murderer* (2016), p. 191.

Eady lived in a house in the same road; in 1944 she was a victim of serial killer John Christie at No. 10 Rillington Place). Although this was in his pre-Poirot days, he did play Inspector Japp in a 1985 TV film of the 1930s Poirot story *Lord Edgware Dies* (set in what were then modern times); Peter Ustinov was Poirot. Suchet said of his acting in it that it was 'possibly the worst performance of his career'. He later played Poirot in a rather better adaptation of the same book. Philip Jackson who played Inspector Japp in the Suchet series lives in Hanwell. The Hoover building on the Western Avenue, Perivale, is used in the television adaptation of the Poirot short story, *The Dream* (from the collection of stories in *The Adventure of the Christmas Pudding*), standing in for a factory where Benedict Farley, an industrialist, is shot dead. The factory is an art deco grade two listed building which now used as a supermarket.

Ealing, therefore, had an influence on Agatha Christie and on her writings. This was due to her regular and lengthy visits to her Auntie-Grannie, Mrs. Margaret Miller, who lived at No. 99 Uxbridge Road from 1881-1914. She spent much of her happy youth at that house. As with Agatha's birthplace, Ashfield, it no longer exists.

Part of Mrs. Miller's character was used for that of Miss Marple, though she did not appear in print until a decade after Mrs. Miller's death. Because of her association with Ealing it is mentioned a few times in her stories and it is thus ironic that the actor who later played the definitive Poirot also lived in the same district.

BIBLIOGRAPHY

Anon, *Ealing Illustrated,* Messrs. G. Tyrer & Co. (1893), 48 pages.

Anon, *Ealing: A County Town near London* (1904), 83 pages.

Christie, Agatha, *An Autobiography,* Collins (1977), ISBN 978-0-00-216012-4, 542 pages.

Harper, Charles G., *Rural Nooks Round London,* Chapman & Hall Ltd. (1907), 194 pages.

Hounsell, Peter, *Ealing and Hanwell Past,* Historical Publications (1991), ISBN 978-0-948667-13-8, 144 pages.

Jones, Charles, *Ealing: From Village to Corporate Town,* S. B. Spaull (1901), 191 pages.

Jones, Charles, *Ealing: A Decade of Progress, 1901-11* (1911), 42 pages.

Morgan, Janet, *Agatha Christie: A Biography,* Harper Collins (1984), ISBN 978-0-00-824395-1, 394 pages.

Oates, Jonathan, *Ealing: A Concise History,* Amberley Publishing (2014), ISBN 978-1-445633-69-5, 126 pages.

Oates, Jonathan, *Foul Deeds and Suspicious Deaths in Ealing,* Wharncliffe Books (2006), ISBN 978-1-845630-12-6, 174 pages.

Oates, Jonathan, *Ronald Chesney: The Middle Class Murderer*, Mango Books (2016), ISBN: 978-1-911273-09-7, 230 pages.

INDEX

A
Acton 14, 16, 31-32, 34, 38, 57.
Adventure of the Christmas Pudding, The (story collection) 58.
Adventure of Hunter's Lodge, The (short story) 53.
And Then There Were None (novel) 22.
Ashfield, Devon 7, 67, 42.
At Bertram's Hotel (novel) 27.

B
Baker, Sarah 51-52.
Baker, Sophia 51-52.
Benbow, Arthur 39, 50-53.
Big Four, The (novel) 55.

C
Castlebar Road 10, 13, 52, 56.
Christie, Agatha, see Miller, Agatha.
Covell, Annie 39, 47-49.
Covell, Edward 48-50.

D
Dream, The (short story) 58.

E
Ealing:
    Cemetery 10-11, 41, 43-45.
    Churches 9-13, 21-22.
    Film studios 7, 38.
    Hospitals 12.
    Parks 11, 13-14.
    Population 9-11, 13, 15.
    Schools 11-13, 16, 45.
    Shops 10, 13, 17, 23, 35, 45.

F
4.50 from Paddington (novel) 57.

G
Greenaway, Devon 7.

H
Hanwell 16, 20, 31, 34, 38, 48-49, 54-58.
Harrogate 7.
Haven Green 11-12, 49, 53-54.

J
Jones, Charles 11-13, 17-18, 22, 32-33.

K
Kingsley Avenue 50-51.

L
Lord Edgware Dies (novel) 58.

M
Mall, The 10, 49.
Marple, Miss Jane 7, 27-28, 57-58.
Miller:
    Agatha 11-12, 16, 18-28, 31, 33-34, 37-39, 41-45, 47, 52-53, 56-58.
    Clarissa 16, 20, 26, 42-43, 45.
    Frederick 16, 20, 26, 41-43, 45.
    Margaret:
        General 7, 16, 19-20, 22-29, 33-34, 38, 42-43, 58.
        Sayings 27-29.
        Servants 25-27.
        Social life 24-26, 38, 42.
Moorby, Agnes 47.
Murder of Roger Ackroyd, The (novel) 43.

N
Newspapers 26, 33-34, 37-38, 41, 44.

O
One, Two, Buckle My Shoe (novel) 56.

P
Perry, George 39, 47-49, 53.
Poirot, Hercule 7, 53-59.

S
Scotcher:
    Annie 47.
    James 47.
Shakespeare, William 7.
Secret of Chimneys, The (novel) 54.
Sleeping Murder (novel) 28.
Suchet, David 57.
Sunningdale, Berkshire 7.

T
They do it with Mirrors (novel) 28.
Torquay 7, 16, 20, 23, 26, 42.

Index

Towards Zero (novel) 57.
Transport 10, 15-17, 31-35, 54.

U
Uxbridge Road 9-10, 22, 31-34, 47, 58.

W
Watts, Margaret 20, 24, 26, 28, 42, 44-45.
World War One 13, 42, 57.

www.ingramcontent.com/pod-product-compliance
Lightning Source LLC
Chambersburg PA
CBHW061250040426
42444CB00010B/2330